Nietzsche's Attaché Case

Daniel Weissbort

NIETZSCHE'S ATTACHÉ CASE

New & Selected Poems

CARCANET

First published in Great Britain in 1993 by
Carcanet Press Limited
208-212 Corn Exchange Buildings
Manchester M4 3BQ

A CIP catalogue record for this book
is available from the British Library.
ISBN 1 85754 023 9

The publisher acknowledges financial assistance
from the Arts Council of Great Britain.

Printed and bound in England by SRP Ltd, Exeter

Acknowledgements:

Some of these poems have appeared in *The Leaseholder* (Carcanet 1971), *In an Emergency* (Carcanet 1972), *Soundings* (Carcanet 1977), *Leaseholder: New and Selected Poems 1965-1985* (Carcanet 1986), *Fathers* (Northern House Poets 1991), and *Inscription* (Cross Cultural Communications 1993). There have been some revisions. Others have appeared in *The Bombay Literary Review, Encounter, PN Review, Stand,* and *The Tel Aviv Review.*

CONTENTS

LAKE

~

SELECTED POEMS

To Carole

LAKE

Of a car creeping across gravel, a bonfire,
of wind in the late autumn foliage,
I don't permit such arid associations
to run their course, to distract me.

I have to set my mind on it and speak the word,
superimpose the image of a lake over those sounds,
and even then, it's only,
overcoming my reticence,
when I go down to stare at the lake that ...

I am standing here, relieved:
the lake's agitation seems to still
the agitation within me.
I'm almost mesmerized by the waves –
at the same time, surface and depth –
that criss-cross in flawless formations.

More elaborate metaphors now crop up.
Yet I'm surprised how often these still have to do with dryness –
for instance, wrinkled sheet, shifting desert sands.
I set them beside the lake's liquidity,
cling to the notion of liquidity,
and stare at the lake.
I try to outstare the metaphors.

Suddenly, over the lake, your last word comes to me,
innocent, unprotesting. Oivey!
You were like a child, scared, shy,
who turns to his parents –
though to whom did you turn?
Certainly not to me, as I bent close,
half lying on the bed, beside you,
concentrating on you as never before,
to catch and retain this summing up.

Your pensive exclamation, father, comes back to me,
as I stand, after sunset, on the shore,
under a feathery sky,
a continent and thirty years away.
And the thought, how long ago it was –
we could be brothers now –
makes my throat contract,
as if those words were mine ...

Well, I am thinking of you,
your strange innocence, your defencelessness,
who set out with hope, deferred rather than abandoned,
but not remembered, even in your dying,
I who stand now at another end of the earth,
scarcely imaginable in your scheme of things.

The lake's lid lifts.
No eye, except mine
that settles there ...
I enter through an open trap,
enter, pulling about me
whisps that I catch on of the air.
Enter and down,
so my head is covered now
and darkness grows,
increasing me.
I can breathe again,
I have come out within.
But there's no light
to guide me.
Only the knowledge, the certainty,
I shall not stumble or fall.
It is within,
within myself, I step.
The knocking is my own heart now,
a distant beat

4

that fades at last ...
Am I wired?
Is the head here, the heart there?
Lamenting my separated heart,
I know it, thus, at once,
back in place.

Gulls, those resolutely legless flyers,
have bustled us off the beach.
From within the house I hear them creak.

When I make to descend again, they scatter –
but slow, reluctant, with a deep resentment,
yielding their place, deferring,
in near rebellion, near refusal.

I am being pressed back, anyway, by the hot wind
that leans against the bluff,
back from slaughter strip where the pickings are so easy.

Where have they gone?
Under what waves did they hide their voices,
in what breeze their gestures?
Where are they dispersed, among what clouds?

Gulls speed by my window,
their shrill calls an offering to the air.
Something has washed up on the shore.
I see them, in my mind's eye, crowd about it,
stiff-legged, sleek heads on the qui vive.

Yesterday, on the promenade,
a raggedy crow lifted and dropped,
lifted and dropped, leading me on,
until I had to laugh, straight into its dark beak.

Again I stare closely at the waters,
and then far out, across.
Gulls' cries come at me through the air,
detached from their utterers,
which dither between water and sky.

The breakers spill gravel onto the grey shore.
I sniff the air. The wind grooms me,
as I stand, eyes closed now, so I might be praying
or meditating – in any case,
unremarkable in such circumstances.

The goldfinches, in their regimentals,
have been plucking bare the giant thistles
we sowed last year, among the "100,000 wild flowers."

So now I'm constantly distracted by birds
that line the wires, taking stock,
then dropping onto the antlered giants.
And what a mess they've made of them!

As for the spikiness,
that seems not to bother them in the least,
those experts whose time has come.

The trees are not quite ready,
yet I shake down their leaves.

That's what I dreamt. Or it is spring,
with a blossom-filled tree and us beneath it,
and someone grabs the trunk and shakes,
and flowers tumble out onto us.
Yet though, like the rest, I laugh,
I also regret this premature bringing down,
even if, for a while, it's like a flower-festival ...

I am distracted, even in my dreams.
When I think of the trees,
or when, as now, thoughts of them simply come,
I am astonished by them!
Yet that inner life persists,
a kind of continuum or peace,
as a man keeps his head down and reads on and on
of beauty and its passing ...

This is not cowardice, nor even
a failure to take reasonable precautions.
Indeed, such inwardness may be the best protection,
when, otherwise, the odds are overwhelming.

You go out upon the ice,
wondering if you're being a fool.
Will it crack?
Will it open up, swallow you, crush you?
Must you claw your way back onto it,
freezing, drag yourself to safety?
No backwoodsman,
no canny habitué of the wilds,
you are uneasy,
as you proceed over the oh-so-fresh expanse,
towards the ice hills.
Every now and then you stop,
turn right around – a full circle –
listen, listen to the silence.

When you stop, it starts.
Did you ever truly listen before?
It is new, but that is what silence is,
always new, each time.
Then you set off again.
The hills approach,
their shadows reach out for you.
And you make your way to the top, to the very edge.
You perch on the edge of those frozen breakers.
You peer over, hoping they'll not disintegrate,
not at that moment when you are standing on them,
taking comfort from your virtual weightlessness, your punyness,
amidst all this musculature.
Then you notice a sound.
It is like a clock ticking.
You turn, set off, back
across the white plain,
stopping every now and then to listen,
to make sure it is still the silence you hear,
and not that other.

The shadows lurch, they ripple
across submerged trunks.
Nature is shouting, silently,
waiting to be rescued,
like Jews assembled in the Platz.
Everybody's waiting.
The guards too. That's us.

So, who gave the orders,
summoned us all? And why
can we do nothing but wait,
trapped always
in this moment, this now,
never to escape, not
into a better world?

I shall take the sun with me,
the sky, the moon,
and the ubiquitous grass, of course.
Verges now lift my spirit most of all,
and beetles in their laden passage under upraised soles
hold my attention.

I shall take the sun
and put it in that sky, the same,
and the grass, into which the beetle plunges,
will continue to cheer me.

Somehow, when I was watching,
nature always backed off!
I'd stare at the lake,
but it had already retreated,
being subtly out of range.
And the wind that stirred the grass
looked past me, confusing my senses.
And as I gazed at distant hills,
they turned away, rather than enfold me.
And even streams would cold-shoulder me!
I so yearned to love nature,
for my love to be reciprocated.
All the time, of course, it was within me,
I was part of it, really.
And this accounts for the perfect bewilderment that was my life.

CATS

Nightly she brings us a shrew or a mouse.
Nightly we convey to her we won't complete the circle:
we order her to drop it, we are adamant.
Next day the corpse is returned to the undergrowth,
eyes delicately closed, pink fingers crooked,
as though they've just finished tying some complicated knot.
She makes corpses, question marks.
Nightly we fail to relieve her of their burden.

It requires all your attention,
to follow death's meticulous instructions.
Not a moment to lose either,
I mean, whatever was undone
must remain forever undone.
Whatever was accomplished up till now
is all that remains after.

As for the creatures,
this cat, for instance,
it's the same story –
he's in death's charge.
We can only watch, touch his nose, his flanks.
In his narrow skull,
there is no more room for us.

It rained.
After a week of sunshine and low humidity –
even the night before, the sky was clear
and you pointed out a star –
it rained all day.

He'd attached himself to us,
one entire flank laid bare,
so we thought he'd been in some dreadful scrap,

but, for all that, not in the least distrustful.
And four years later, after a "successful" operation,
he just stopped eating and drinking,
until finally we gave up struggling on his behalf.

As I said, it was raining,
raining as we took him to the vet,
raining as we returned without him,
and still raining at dusk.

And it entered my head.
or rather, the words slipped out before I'd had time to think:
"Actually, being a cat
was only one of his personae."

And immediately I thought:
That's not what I wanted to say at all.
And I wondered why I'd said it,
or what had.

All I could recall was
picking, or rather, scooping them up,
several of the mice that scattered ...
Also a volelike creature, eyeless,
which crouched, unmoving,
and, smaller still, another
which, if lifted, must bruise dreadfully ...
Meanwhile, the cats had gathered, lunging,
as I tried to fend them off.
And I caught a glimpse of darkness about their mouths,
as though bits of their own gut hung there,
or a kind of vomit, but was able to transport
two handfuls of miscellaneous rodents
to the door, opening it, and releasing them.
Each heart-beating I felt distinctly in my palm,
remembering how, many years before,

a mouse which I had rescued from a cat,
sank its needle teeth into my thumb,
and I flung it murderously to the ground ...
Meanwhile the vole blindly made for the open,
but the mice doubled back,
eager to return to the warmth.
And I tried to chase them off again,
knowing they'd give me the slip
and find the cats that lay in wait.

I had forgotten how light they were, kittens,
before I dreamed of them again,
a rapid dream, in half sleep,
between waking and waking,
woken by the sustained squealing,
the furious whirling of one I'd evidently stepped on,
even as I was exclaiming: "Oh, you've got kittens!"
stooping to pick one up, and at the same time thinking,
this is the second litter and how will you find homes,
or will they be done away with?
By now its siblings, consolatory, had gathered about the hurt one,
my guilt too urging it to have done,
and, embarrassed, hoping nobody would realize I was the cause,
I bent to lift the single straggler, deserted, barely visible
        by my feet,
a black-and-white, when the others were shades of brown,
no doubt the runt of that little mob,
that had barely woken into life,
slow and stumbling, bewildered,
which I would make the gift of a few moments warmth and
        tenderness again,
stroke its dry little nose, its worried cat's brow,
between dozy eyes that blinked and blinked.
I who lifted it now gently in my palms
had forgotten how light they were, kittens.

THE GATE

He had much to tell me,
but he never got round to it,
though he continued to smile.
It's his smile I remember now,
as though he were waiting
for just the right moment to make me a gift
of what he'd collected for me.
He'd plans for me,
yet he never consulted me about them.
He just kept on smiling –
we'd never really talked –
with increasing inwardness,
musing, wanting the best for me.

There was that one time, though –
he died in August –
when we sat, sunning ourselves, in Regent's Park ...
With his eyes closed, absently, head tilted back,
he remarked that nature was wonderful.
It was something as plain, as ordinary as that,
but which rose from so deep within him,
the words barely touched it.
And first I thought he was just thinking aloud.
I felt embarrassed, as if I'd eavesdropped,
and even though his eyes were closed,
I looked away ...

Later, much later, I realized
it was me he was talking to,
me he was addressing.
It seems, he had forgotten for the moment
who I was.

It didn't happen to us, so
it didn't happen. My father,
on his fleshless legs, tottering

to the bathroom, but
it was in his own home, from his own bed,
not bare ground, tiered bunks.
It didn't happen to us.
The tide of death stopped short,
well short, of us,
and then retreated,
as it had to,
as it surely had to,
so I might grow into myself,
the self that waited for me.

I am what those young folk, my parents,
in their hasty, youthful fashion,
between coping mainly with one another, I suppose,
made me.

When I think of them now,
they seem to be preparing for an invasion,
moving large objects about,
as though erecting
a barricade. Or maybe
building a pyre?

Or else he's on his knees before the cocktail-altar,
with its interior bottlescape,
and his arm outstretched: benedictus benedicat.
And she's making the rounds –
how else should I put it! –
going from one to another,
in just such a manner, insouciant,
as she lit the candles on our birthday cake,
which we tried, with our own laughter, to make a meal of.

But who will answer for this festive time?
For they are long gone, long about
their undone business gone.

She, it was, slipped past him,
though they remembered this only when someone remarked:
"Has dad been told?"
They were not even sure where he was,
though it took only a moment to remember
that he was still alive.
"Yes, he has been told."
"He has been told?"
"Yes, he has been told."
"And how did he take it?"
The answer was indistinct, just as he,
the vision of him conjured up by this,
was vague, cobweb-draped,
of a man so old he could be left out of the reckoning.
She too.
"The worst is, there is so much to do,
so many loose ends ..."
But, of course, there weren't –
that was the worst of it.

"Come to tea with the children," she'd say.
And occasionally I managed it.
She was delighted then, cheerful, brisk,
despite her fourscore years.
She kept biscuits and choc-ices to encourage them.

But after a while they lost interest,
and I lost my power to persuade them.
And in the end they hardly came at all.
I would seek out the biscuits for myself.
They were stale but sweet.

It almost happened!
She was there. I was there.
And I knew how to do it.
But somehow she was not looking in the right direction.
And somehow I waited too long.
And somehow, when it came to it,
I wasn't really sure I knew.
And somehow, she didn't seem to realize I was there even.
And then I fell into a reverie.
And meanwhile she vanished.
And, actually, I didn't know enough in any case.
Yiddish is harder than that.

Silenced! The thought obsesses me.
Wasn't it enough she could not longer sing "Élie, Élie!"
She'd prepare as usual, clearing her throat,
but a tremulousness was all that came out.
Yet while the rest of her had aged past the point of mattering,
her speaking voice had remained young and strong.
Businesslike, determined, deep and vigorous,
it cancelled the oceanic gap between us.
Now it was as though someone had stuffed it in a bag
and walked off.
    Outraged, I cry: "Bring it back!"

If it was good form
to always leave something on one's plate,
you didn't see the point of it.
The point was to never quit.
And in the end, there'd be nothing for them to brag about,
there'd be nothing left for them,
every last scrap of you would have been consumed.

I think you're living on,
so you can be looked after,
and so they can look after you –
everyone's getting what he needs.

Now you know for sure
you weren't going to be left to your own devices,
God is good after all.

You grin a lot, trying out:
b ... b ... m ... m ... d ... d ...
You can be a good little girl now,
without ever having to grow up again.

You're en route now – the "Ship of Death."
You're making the crossing, who all your life
feared that passage.
With your one year of schooling, you now know more
than I, your "son the professor"!

The ship you boarded is afloat,
the journey has begun at last.
In the exhilaration of the sailing,
nostalgia has simply ceased to exist.

No longer terra firma underneath,
but a voice, a breathing, a lifting up,
everything starting over again ...

The one you were would regret this leavetaking,
but you are no longer who you were.
Having forgotten to return,
you have remembered what none of us
remembers till the journey has begun.

You had a companion,
a faithful sitter by your side.

Like the mother-needy infant,
your soul received the succor
it required.

She could not depend
on the natural inclination of people to protect their old.
But then she never admitted she was old.
Instead she went on adding locks to her doors.

I imagined her locking herself away for good one day.
Instead of that,
she did what, not being there, I cannot quite picture:
came out from behind her locks,
handed herself over into the safekeeping of others.

It's not fair or kind,
but still, I'm glad I never saw it!
In memory of her, I call to mind
a valiant *châtelaine*.

It's raining,
as you say goodbye to me.
Outside your kitchen window, rain.
You pay no attention –
after all, you hardly ever go out now.
The rain falls anyway.
In eighty-five years you've seen a lot of it!
It rains, or the sun shines ...
Anyway it's reassuring,
it means at least you're not dead!

But what am I thinking!
It wasn't raining when we said goodbye.
Only now the rain
rustles across my roof,
drums soothingly on it as though on canvas,
enters my memory of that last time too.

I talked to her through the coffin sides.
It's not true that the spirit departs in a rush.
The coffin was literally where her spirit was too.
And meanwhile the rabbi intoned his prayers.
As background music, it was just right.

Her silence was eloquent.
There was no need for words.
All she needed was some reassurance from me,
telling her that I knew she was there.
She wasn't so frightened, but still needed me
to tell her I knew.

It was a mercifully long walk to the family plot.
We're visiting daddy again, this year,
the three of us, as we used to do,
I told her, except that you
are on the other side, as they say!
But we'll soon be joining you anyway.
So don't you worry. I can tell you things now..
For instance, that operation I had, it was cancer.
Or maybe you knew!

So, we were able to talk freely,
like many years ago.
We talked, or I talked for both of us,
never more freely than on this walk,
with her riding in state.

It was peaceful.
Not sad so much
as a time to speak your mind.
And when they lowered her,
it wasn't solemn,
but funny, yes!
And I said to her:
Don't you think it's funny,
with us peering down at you,
and you lying there,
looking up!
And first she said:
I'm not so sure about that!
I'm a bit scared, you know.
And then I asured her:
You needn't be, though!
And she listened to me.

Then the rabbi, as he'd promised he would,
said a prayer for daddy.
I'd liked that idea –
and she approved too,
because daddy was there.
I wasn't quite sure where,
but he seemed less unpresent than usual,
less unpresent even than he'd used to be,
in fact so excited to have his wife again,
he could hardly contain himself, although
she was too busy looking about her –
it was all so new –
to pay much attention to him for the moment.

And then we trooped back up the path.
She let me talk to the others, to play the host,
confident that I'd be there for her, if needed.
We'd had such a grand time on that walk.

I am trying to find her –
it's a matter of death! –
wherever she may be,
trapped on some cliff ledge,
or wandering lost in the fog.
I am trying to find her –
can you help me?
And if I succeed,
I shall steady her, reasure her,
I shall calmly lead her to safety.
She's not scared exactly,
just confused, just lost.
I can guide her, she's not wandered far,
remain with her, set her on the path,
the path she'll not stray from again.
And it's there I shall say goodbye,
where the path starts.
Because if I say anything now,
she'll not hear,
it will be like speaking to myself,
when I ought to be looking for her.

She was a kind of me, although
she didn't know it as I did.
And so, as I watched her breaking down,
it was as if I watched myself.
Instead of offering sympathy,
I tried to prop her up,
to resurrect her in the flesh.
It was unkind of me, but then
she was a kind of me.

I want to love your death!
I don't want just to let it pass away.

I want to play.
I want my knowing consummated.
I want your dying to stand still,
so I can size it up,
so I can embody it, body it.
I don't want it to go away,
to go the way of all death.
I don't want it just to go away,
as though it had forgotten me,
as though I had forgotten it.
Not until I've taken a chunk out of it,
not until we've divided it between us.

I missed you.
You're on your way to some far corner of somewhere.
How should I have guessed,
when you'd not moved in years?
Suddenly you disposed of
that inefficient envelope, your body,
and simply took off.
I'm telling you, it hurts!
I'm left here,
searching in my mind
for where you went.
But you're already too far,
I don't recognize you any more.
For one thing, it's so unlike you,
taking off this way.
Why, when I used to go out,
didn't you always want to know where I was going!
Yet now you've gone,
without a word as to where –
you didn't even tell me when you left.
Yet I cannot find it in my heart
to blame you. Besides,
two can play at that game!

The flat is waiting for her to come back.
All her things are in place.
But I feel their uneasiness.
For too long already, they've not been handled by her,
and now here's someone else
picking up and peering
at what was only for her eyes.
Even if, reverently, I replace each object,
it doesn't take kindly to my meddling,
wants to shake off the feel of me.

Dust has grown everywhere.
Within moments my hands are black.
And when I've done – the havoc!
The flat will never be the same again.
Even so the message hasn't yet got through.
Oh, when is she coming back!
The flat can't stand it:
After all these years,
how could she do this to me!

But the truth is, in the end, she ran
from her forty years of life here,
threw a few articles into a bag,
and left, not even closing cupboard doors behind her.
The flat, a deserted lover, won't believe the facts,
but tells how she just went away for a while,
stubbornly repeats:
She'll be back ... She'll be back ...

I did it for me. Still,
at the back of my mind was the thought we might speak.
Here was something we could do together as well.
But you died!
"A real Yiddishe moma!" the rabbi cried,
in his preposterous encomium.

Yet he was right. You were.
Of course, I hadn't any longer hoped to practise on you –
you'd got too old for that.
But here was something we might do.
We'd have had a few laughs, in any case,
as I struggled to find my way back to being a Jew.

Her voice, silenced was like
another body by her side in bed.
She tried to point it out,
to include it in the conversation,
but it couldn't adjust to this kind of a separation.
It felt self-conscious, ugly, raw.
It wasn't meant to function on its own at all.
It felt like something shapeless –
a bladder, a flayed carcass maybe,
a blind beast dredged from the bottom of the sea.
And she, almost weightless, with it lying there,
hung on to it now, like ballast,
or a giant teddy bear.

My eyes are drawn to the woman's hands,
clenching, as the man,
visibly more infirm than she,
levers himself from his seat.
They have reached this late point in life together,
but what keeps him going now
is more her will than his own.
He is adrift here,
high over the Atlantic,
as he'll soon be adrift ...
And I think of my mother's journey –
a quarter of a century without her spouse –
which has just ended,
and of that youngish man, my father.

Now that she's stopped moving,
I can sketch her,
now that she's keeping still,
I can plant myself in front of her
and study her, get her right at last.

But I've not done so yet.
What am I waiting for?
Her features are a bit of a blur
and I am aware mainly
of my own inward look and idle hands.

Now she has joined those others,
inaudible. (To us, that is. God knows
what tales they tell among themselves!)
Now if I bring her back,
what shall I be bringing back?

I break into boxes, scrutinize chests,
sift through your life's debris,
separating the necessary from the unnecessary ...

You were quite orderly,
but you kept everything that looked official,
as though it possessed value.
In a sense, it does.

Still, I'm the family historian, not the state's.
I dispose of cartons of bank records,
of decades-old tax form duplicates,
of share dividend receipts.

At last I'm getting to look into your things.
I've dug right down to the bottom
and have uncovered buried treasure
that is no longer treasure.

I'm bringing it all back anyway,
up to the surface,
where you no longer preside.

I pretend this doesn't concern you.

Had I pressed her, would she
have maintained
that God exists?

I think not.

Yet the rituals were a comfort to her.
She did not question them.
But God, who needs him!

I walk from room to room.
What has become of the spirit of the place?
If I throw my eye out of focus,
or only half concentrate,
it's as if nothing was altered –
the furniture, what's left,
still where it was before,
general impression the same,
that is if I ignore
the bare surfaces, pictureless walls,
in particular the absence of a phone on the bureau in the hall.
I stare long at the bureau.
How much has to be taken away
before a place, finally, gives up the ghost?
And now that everything is ready, waiting,
suspended, emptied, loosed,
I am astonished by
the density of dust, shimmering in the air,
where sunlight cuts through.

Oh, it's May the First again!
And for the third time in a row,
again no *muguet* from mother ...

For a while, during her middle years,
mother would send me a card, with lily-of-the-valley.
Sometimes she'd even put sweet smelling muguet in my room.

Tonight the TV News will blend
tanks and missiles jerking through Red Square.
I shall have come to the end
of yet another uneasy *anniversaire*.

C'est ta fleur, mother would repeat,
year after year.
But still it never sank in.

The moon was unsolicitous,
impersonal, indifferent.
It had merely chanced, unknowing, on my corner,
illuminating me ...

Not like when I was ill, feverish,
and soon the attendant's moonlike face hung there,
asking questions.

Though how was I able to answer, with half my jaw gone
and my tongue plugging the gap?
Anyway, I was as pleased as punch,
like when Isakowicz the dentist
congratulated me, boychik,
promising he'd eat his hat,
because I bore the pain so uncomplainingly.
But really, there was very little pain.

Yes, in the recovery room, there I felt safe.

But the moon, which had been pale and ulcerous in the afternoon,
last night shone brusquely in at my window,
as though mother had switched on the light
to see if I slept soundly, or because she didn't care.

Or perhaps we had to move,
perhaps the enemy was at the gate!

VALEDICTION

You sit, blinking intelligently:
So, when's something going to be done about it!
But you're patient too.
For a time, you look around,
waiting for us to get organized.
Tolerantly you let us manhandle you, shift your legs,
press down on your jerking knee,
stuff a pillow behind your head.
You look around, tactfully,
as though it all had nothing to do with you,
your mind on other things.
Won't you let us in on the secret?
Here we're busying ourselves about you,
and meanwhile you've the air of a saint or martyr,
utterly inaccessible, indifferent.
Our faces float in and out,
like lanterns in a breeze.
But you make no move,
either to duck or push them aside.
Not meeting our eyes,
you seem to be listening to
something else – though not particularly.
Whatever we do, you just blink.
Are you counting, calculating,
is your head filled with some complicated reckoning?
Is that what occupies you?
Or are you solving a cosmic mystery!
We half expect you suddenly to look up,
that is to look up at us,
rise to your feet, nod and say:
"Alright, enough's enough!"
Instead, though you don't mean anything by it,
you've no time for us.
But what is so pressing elsewhere?
How do we get you to notice us again?
Should we stand on our heads,
should we dance naked in front of you!
Finally, we're reduced to talking amongst ourselves.

We review the situation –
And then we start over again,
stroking your hand, squeezing it,
touching your face, looking
into your still eyes that occasionally blink.
Now and again your left hand strays.
Now and again, meaningfully,
you squeeze the hand holding yours.
You scratch your cheek,
finger your jaw,
adjust your glasses,
tug familiarly at an eyelid.
Now and again you even make a brisk gesture in the air,
as though summoning someone,
or looking for a word,
or just beating time.

You had shut up house.
They were standing around, looking at you,
or stroking your hand, your cheek.
That was the easy part.

Later, you opened your eyes,
you had returned.
From time to time, you smiled.
Once or twice you squeezed my hand.

In the end, if you became a burden.
it also dawned on you, perhaps,
that even in these circumstances
you'd a say in the matter.

I'm assuming you wanted to die.
At least, that's what you did.
And how else could you still say goodbye?
Goodbye, my friend!

By the time I got there,
he'd literally had all the stuffing knocked out of him,
with that great dent in his temple where they went in
and rummaged around with their tools.
He seemed to be concentrating, as far as he was able,
taking a good hard look at the damage.
And I guess he decided – I like to think I'd have too –
that not enough was left to make a go of it.
So, he lingered, as he had to,
while the medics went through their repertoir,
knowing in the end their attention must flag,
and that then his opportunity would arrive.
And it did. After a while, he sneaked off,
and shut the door behind him, just in case ...

Well, that's how it seemed to me.
I know it probably wasn't that way at all.
Probably, what was left of him
was straining to make the best of a bad job,
to fit together, like it always had, to start building again.
The doctors and technicians co-operated,
using all their science and art
to interpret what was going on,
to encourage, stimulate, and clear away the obstacles.
Probably, it was just touch and go
whether he'd make it in the end.
That he didn't, that he didn't make it,
was simply one of those things ... probably.

Did you weep,
as I said goodbye,
maybe for the last time?
Your left eye watered.
Was that weeping?

Were you angry?
When I tried to find more words after that,
you merely looked aside
(If you're going, go!)
Was that anger?

Kultur is what you'd cherished:
order, authority, justice,
everything *en place*;
a ruler alert to the barbarian,
ever-present at the gate.
Examples of this primal struggle,
of the human intelligence,
resisting the mischievous forces of disorder,
you found elsewhere, for instance
at an exhibition of Cartier-Bresson,
pausing before a portrait of Camus
and drawing my attention to
the intelligence in that face.
Such intelligence you saw as well –
and made me see –
in the stone face of Sumerian Gudea, Ensi, Governor,
and painstakingly constructed an epic poem,
concerning his struggle with the Guti,
those who'd demolish, not preserve,
who'd substitute their own unprincipled rule
for sober legality, founded on ...
Founded on what? You championed
the time-bound, time-affirming truths,
against the new, experimental, even visionary,
since risk-taking was no virtue,
the stakes being too high to justify it,
especially now. Did they ever?
You were convinced that justice
was an attribute of intelligence,
that it could not be legislated,

only protected from assault.
The alternative being so far worse,
you did not doubt the effort was worthwhile.
Expecting no commendation, no reward,
you hoped only for the survival of your side.

As I prepare to write about the rain,
I remember how you admired
my image of rain entering the ground "with soft feet."
It doesn't sound so good now, as I say it!
Yet you commended me upon my "daring,"
though even then I felt I'd somehow
taken unfair advantage of you
who were so measured, so orderly.
As I sit in this dry space, surrounded by the rain,
in front, scarcely visible through pine and birch, the lake,
as I sit here, in this fluvial universe,
I think too of Edward Thomas,
and of his poems about the rain,
how it dissolves all human accoutrements.
Indeed, today, out walking,
my clothes clinging to me
and water dripping from hair, nose, ears,
it was as if I were dissolving into the ground,
rather than striding over it
to where I now sit, thinking about you.

Since I started writing today, he hasn't moved.
Well, I'm trying, still trying!
I keep coming back to him, as he stands beside her –
and now I think of it, they're about the same height –
a little uncomfortably, a little prematurely too,
so I can't just treat them the same way.
For one thing, I haven't the heart to! After all,

he was my friend, like an older brother,
a mentor, a disciple too.
The truth is, it's breaking my heart!
It's like in those last months, when I tried
to find words ordinary enough
to cancel his extraordinary agony,
tried to pitch my voice so low
it would penetrate the din of his outraged faculties,
cajoled, manipulated, appealed
to his sense of fair play, attempted blackmail,
telling him I loved him too. And still
I feel there's something I didn't try,
that somehow I failed him, though I know
not only does he not blame me,
but it is presumptuous to suppose I might have succeeded
when others, far closer to him, failed.
Bearing no grudge, he stands now,
blinking in his usual manner,
and waits alongside her and the others,
hands awkwardly, ingratiatingly clasped in front,
as in that bust of his beloved Gudea.

WORDS

I have arrived ahead of my words.
Those I use are mute,
they do not even look at me.
They are unborn,
unwoken from their sleep,
and not to be hastened.
But I am impatient.
I prop them up,
arrange them in ranks.
They stand, an inert host,
like a toy army, silence hovering above them.
And I move them about.
I am reluctant to leave them,
cannot tear myself away –
they are so many.
I caress them, cajole them.
I talk to them, separate them,
break up their ranks.
But still they do not respond.
At best they remind me now
of certain moments of gratification.
I am playing games with them,
musical games, abstract games.
I concentrate on the harmonies, the progressions:
it takes my mind off them.
I almost forget them.
There is, there is in all things
a melodic essence, could we but grasp it.
And that is the eternal life.
But, then, I raise my eyes,
and the words, drab, neglected,
no longer engage me.
The music I thought I heard,
dies out in the air,
having nowhere to go.
I have arrived ahead of my words.

I begin again: Must, Have to,
Must, Have to; Ought, Should,
Should, Ought. I experiment with:
Shall, Will. And then back to Must etc.

Exhortation gets me nowhere!
The desire for change must arise from within,
spontaneously, so to speak –
Must again!

What shall I do with all the Musts and Shoulds?
How shall I distract them, finally?

I keep them at bay with questions,
lie down, sleep with questions.
I awake, reaching for a question,
get up questioning.

"When was it not too late?"
The literal question, not the exclamation.

You can open boxes with it.
You can open your breast.
But the pain you feel then is all that's left,
it's the desert you may come to love.

You approach at great risk.
What words will it chose, lethal?
How big will it grow, larger than you?
Where will it go, within you?

You open your mouth for more air, or –
as one opens a door inside a sealed building –
for the illusion of air.

Yes, open your mouth
and remain that way,
not moving anymore,
so that this, too, is suspended.

A grimace – the closest you can come to ecstasy.

As I read them aloud,
the words stir a little.
I try not to agitate them.
I accustom them gradually to my voice,
not waking them abruptly,
if possible not waking them at all,
only, perhaps, causing them some dream perturbation.

In this way, I am able finally even
to shout without rousing them.
I shout them. And if they turn over at that,
it is only to sleep more soundly.

I was trying to find the words ...
"In a flash, it all comes back, sort of,
the place itself, people, relationships, the intensity,
      it all comes together, see ..."
He was unimpressed, skeptical, as he used to be,
before the bourgeois world, in a manner of speaking,
      wore him down.
But, in any case, I suppose what I really meant was,
youth does, and I knew it all the time,
but couldn't be so banal, because
it wasn't quite that either, more
regret, incredulity, not being able to accept it was over,
before I'd had a chance to live it according to my precepts,
just as now I could not find words to convince,

though it was evident too that I'd provided him
with an opportunity to display his former feistiness.
After which, wordless again, we both looked about us
at the panelling, which I now saw was suspiciously rough,
and the interestingly named places on the map,
       which must disappoint.

They point with their eyes.
Uneasily I continue to perform.
I assume there's nothing personal in it,
that they don't mean to be unfriendly.
I continue, and now, occasionally, they turn to each other:
I cannot hear the air-conditioner,
the creak of sneakers, of desks and chairs.
I do hear my finger tap-tapping,
my intake of breath between words,
those words, those unruly words,
that are always threatening to break out.

Language, let out of its cage,
suddenly was everywhere,
smiling, sniffing the air.

Those who fawned,
who danced attendance,
who barely kept their own end up,
were, after all, your paymaster.
And you were doing a job
they tolerated. That is,
together you defined
what tribute must be paid.

Coexistence seemingly's a *sine qua non*.
There's room for exclusive tyrannies,

enough space in between or screens tall enough.
That eager, smiling animal knows it,
or thinks it does, nudging us,
its snout now up between our buttocks.

The city looks into the mirror,
tightens its knot,
turns this way and that,
gives its hair a pat.

Now it is set, as satisfied
as it is ever going to be.
And traffic circulates already,
and already the news vendors are taking up their stations,
and we are about to withstand
the presumptuous onslaught of the nations.

We are preparing to go about our business,
as though nothing threatened our hallowed ways.
We will insist on changelessness,
our heads will, our mouths shall proclaim it,
while creeping in from the outer suburbs,
hugging the ground like poison gas ...

It were a fool who'd name it!

Nemesis walked into my office, holding forth
highmindedly on his concern for words:
language, slack or energetic?
But I stood fast.
The important thing, I said,
is the passion that informs language,
commitment. But, oh, how I hate
the prissy, bullying overtones of that!

What I really wanted to say to him was:
If *you* care enough,
language will take care of *itself*.
The noise that accompanies falling water, Lawrence called it.
But somehow that didn't seem to fit the bill.
No, I knew there was more to it,
or, at least, more that needed to be said.
I knew what he meant, I guess –
Language *is* the test, it's how you *tell*.
And being able to tell's
the trick that we call, well,
having the gift.

All the same, it *is* a trick!
That, finally, is what I wanted to convey ...
Yes, but how do you argue with genius, or nemesis?

As they grow,
as their silence grows too,
I begin to falter –
to hesitate, sometimes to stumble.
My moment is subsumed
in something larger,
though I still hold on to a token,
along with that consciousness
which no longer seems paramount.
Nothing's been changed;
only words have become
counters, more obedient,
less wilful, less autonomous.
Nothing has changed,
except I begin to recognize hot air
when I hear it, lip service
when I pay it.

Visibility takes getting used to.
Keeping an eye out
for the panhandler's tilt,
the telltale lurch,
you find yourself giving old ladies a wide berth,
suspiciously scanning aged men from top to toe.
Voices are fended off, no looking back.
You enter dark alleys with a prayer,
with a vote of thanks emerge from them into a penumbra
that seems like home.
Briefly, then, you are anonymous.
But soon you are once more beacon and body,
once more unignorable.
And even if you anticipate the stage directions,
you sense hands making for you,
flapping themselves across, like bats.
You ask yourself: What became of all their owners?
But you know the answer already: Fear!
Fear brushed them from the canvas.
Increasingly, it is only you who figure here,
who fill this world with your words of description.
They are your words, yours!

Whatever is spoken
has an authenticity
derived from that,
from the fact that it is spoken.
A permanence, a non-ephemerality, results from that,
from its being released,
made susceptible to shaping forces,
to being added to.
Whatever is spoken by us
more deeply roots us.
What we speak instructs us,
no sooner spoken, is wiser than us.

The dead do not cry out –
that's mere wishful thinking.
The dead wait for words to be put into their mouths.
They wait, patiently, obediently,
in that last attitude you chose for them.
But since you are constrained to find the right words,
you wish it were otherwise,
and sometimes you substitute dreams,
in which they speak to you,
prophetic dreams,
though the prophesies themselves may well be false.
Actually, it's those words which, waking,
you invest them with, that count;
words somehow picked from the sealed room,
or sweated through its walls,
reassembled, molecule by molecule;
yes, those, painstakingly precipitated,
not the dream flow,
with its marvellously allusive messages.

STRANGE EVIDENCE

The war mothered us,
sang us lullabies,
spoiled us.
Never again were we so looked after.

We were all orphaned,
we the war generation,
in one fell swoop!
We had not realized –
no one told us –
it was only temporary,
eventually would pack up and move on.
And when, later, we heard of it,
in other places,
we were filled with nostalgia.
Even now when we hum its half remembered tunes,
our eyes mist over.
Sentimentality, you might suppose,
but what did we know of childhood, except war?

And what did we know of war, except childhood?
Happily we played in its precincts,
feeling protected, mostly,
putting to the back of our minds,
or converting into a game,
that we might come to grief.
Our childish terror was out in the open,
shared by all.

And perhaps it was we who kept everyone resolute,
since we believed what we were told,
that notwithstanding the nearness of the threat,
our side must prevail,
the Hun would be defeated, because –
well, because he was a bully and a coward.

We played parts, swapping good and bad,
crayonned airplanes, pluming from the blue,
like fighter pilots, decorating the corner of our page with swastikas.

But now I wonder, did we really feel so safe?
The vision of houses – *houses*, after all –
stove in, the morning after,
even if we romped around in them ...

So, it is with equal longing that I recall
The Donkey Serenade, the Belgian beaches just before the war,
and after, too, those same beaches, and the blockhouses
    we explored,
with their passageways and smelly chambers,
slit windows squinting back across the Channel.

It was fun to drop dried peas
onto pedestrians, four stories below!

One time, a pea I dropped landed in the pipe
of the café-owner, as he stood
smoking outside his place.
He looked around, then up,
and we'd just the time, the maid and I,
to pull our heads back,
though perhaps he saw us anyway,
because he shook a fist goodnaturedly in our direction.

It still seems like a miracle! But, of course,
I can't really be sure,
even if odd things do happen,
like when my aunt's fatal coronary targeted my heart too ...

That little refugee maid –
now I remember, Irene was her name –
was laughing even harder than I was,

as we ducked out of sight. I suppose,
she was scarcely more than a child herself.

I note that my appeals to the Lord
are growing more frequent.

When my mind seems to be fully engaged,
trying to formulate a strategy,
or figure out the opposition,
suddenly I find myself calling on Him,
asking for His help.

I remember how once I was punished for scribbling
        in my textbook.
I didn't protest. I assumed I'd deserved my punishment.
Or perhaps I was too startled to protest or question.

"Hame" was what I wrote, over and over.
Hame? Was it "Home" I had in mind,
or the Hebrew letter "Hem,"
or "Chem," rather,
which stands for Chaim, Life?

It was a compulsion already.
Only, now I am more articulate.

I'll start with the door, the oak,
waiting behind it
for his footsteps in the echoing stairwell,
then his brisk knocking.
I'll start with that –
the waiting. Never too long,
though sometimes, sometimes
he didn't, didn't come at all.

Sometimes I remained,
with my small Hovis loaf,
my tin of baked beans,
and my LPs: Vaughan Williams,
Vittoria de los Angeles,
Greco, Brassens ...
with, outside, the Cambridge darkness,
a few streetlamps,
and occasional footsteps, but not his by now.
And apart from that, just the shadows,
the moving shadows of trees,
and the wind, the wind.
And I must have heard, as well,
the roar of waters by the mill.

Inside the metal box,
with its protective sheen,
was her voice, and the coins
stacked to measure time by.
Outside, night hedged it round,
the wind treated it rough.
I stood, illuminated,
as in a surrealistic painting,
in this box, carefully selected,
on the very edge of town,
and talked to her whose distance from me
made my head ache, willing her
to take the pain away.

Thirty-five years have passed.
She is nothing to me now.
But I still sense the surging wind,
the impatient night without.

They permitted me to amble on their lawns,
to walk beside, to boat upon, their river,
to carouse in their public houses ...
Or else I simply wasn't noticed in the crowd.

But, anyway, I never learnt the ropes.
My short term passed and finally
unequipped and untransformed,
I stepped gingerly down
and instantly was carried off
and out of earshot.

No one explained what had gone wrong.
No one told me where I was, or where I'd been.
Were it not for the evidence,
that strange evidence,
I would not know.

Waiting outside the school
for her to be returned to me
each day: Questions, Questions.
She'd answer wildly, absently,
shouting to friends, her glances
skittering off in all directions,
until finally she settled for me.
And I too settle for something:
a false gay note enters my voice.

Nearly always you are first,
the remains of last night's bread on the table,
the curtains still drawn.
Perhaps you'd been wondering
what they were all up to –
were they planning a revolution?

had they left home? –
and putting down your book,
the one you'd started reading or writing,
you'd made for the kitchen.
Now there is creaking up above.
Actually, you've only just beaten them to it,
your daughters in their short shifts,
rubbing their eyes.

You'll be just the same,
having disposed of the last vestiges of me.
You'll delight in being just the same,
having shaken the dust of me off.
And I'll be just the same.
We'll both be just the same,
grinning, like a pair of blasted idiots!

What guided him wasn't love,
but it was what came his way.
And since he couldn't be sure anything else would,
he was reconciled to it. Besides,
he'd no choice.

And when, later, love –
no mistaking it this time –
entered his life,
naturally he heeded it,
and changed course.

Actually, he had already changed course.
I am standing on the brink, he thought,
of a beautiful old age, surely that
cannot disappoint,
                           though he at last knew,
it is more blessed to give.

You send me vulgar postcards
that mockingly raise the spectre of
that sweating, grunting beast,
with you, cheerful, enthusiastic,
strenuously orgasmic.

So, one day, maybe we'll limp off together,
wriggling our shrunken behinds,
down the false perspective of a painted avenue.

Since my jaw was truncated
and my tongue sectioned,
I've not been able to whistle tunes.
Not unless, with two fingers,
I hold my mouth in place –
and even then ...

Before, I used to whistle like, yes,
like a nightingale, a flute!
Now even the simple family whistle,
I'd have a hard time tootling. (Lord,
let me not be lost in a crowd!)

Well, but nearly all of the family's dead,
and I've surely enough force left in my lips
to produce a windy replica
the remnant might still know me by.

Miniature pterodactyls slide and bank in the sky.
Blossoming trees hold their breath till bursting point.

I grind my teeth and remain within
my unexploded head.

Flying beetles
haul their heavy butts,
like gigantic pregnancies:
they pause, then plunge to earth,
· where they crawl about, stunned,
waiting for the next thing.

I am waiting for the next thing.
I pass the time trying to figure out
what is expected of me.
It still astonishes me that anything is.

I do not know if I have survived.

If I understood him correctly, he said
that the image itself perpetuates the evil it represents,
that through its image, evil retains a sort of actuality.
What, I wondered, are we to do about it then?
Suppress all images?
And, indeed, he mentioned too
the Biblical injunction against idols, against images,
as though this helped confirm his hypothesis:
the evidence, then, of human atrocities, carefully preserved,
at the same time promoting, in a sense embodying,
that which it commemorates.

Yes, what is to be done?
Are we to advance, without memories?
Is that what I heard him say,
that the nightmare we bring along with us must one day be realized,
and so we must lay it down, as a defeated army its arms?
Was he, perhaps, averring that this is the path leading
        to perfection,
to the elimination of all evil?
Is this, then, the solution that,
from just after the beginning,
has eluded us?

On the blue and golden eve
of yet another venture along the route,
not yet quite overgrown,
between my this and my that,
I pause, long enough to draw breath,
not more – not long enough to take my pulse,
or look about me, note
what I've forgotten. Forgotten?
Abandoned, rather, in as orderly a fashion
as hope all will remain there undisturbed
can muster, awaiting my problematical return,
mangled maybe by the whirling arms.
For I shall then resume,
with yet another journey small within,
no loose ends showing,
in the perpetual enlargment which
increasingly turns our walls to water.

Each day I man my ancient battlements,
get wearily up upon them –
at least I'm vertical!
I plod from point to point,
take stock of my defences,
rob Peter to pay Paul.
One thing I know for sure,
there is no hope of reinforcements,
the walls are crumbling,
all's patch and make do, nothing lasts.
Each day I man my battlements,
dream up strategies, ploys,
ways to distract, divert, mislead,
to create an illusion of success,
in the very presence of defeat to celebrate.

I have sentenced myself to
regularly tramping around my old haunts.
No wonder people look at me askance,
my contemporaries, my former associates.
Sensibly, they prefer now to conserve their own energies.

Yesterday, sheltering from the rain
in the doorway of the Holborn Public Library,
standing there in my damp shoes,
staring at the pockmarked street,
I cursed myself for not having anticipated the rush-hour.

Finally I made it home, and in time
for a film by Agnes Varda: The Vagabond.
It's about a girl who takes to the road,
her encounters, her miserable, loveless death.

I'm challenged by the flies,
running rings round each other.
They are dark little demons,
floating on end.

How they vanish in a flash,
snatching themselves away,
and then reappear elsewhere,
appear and reappear!

I allow my eye to follow the flies more closely.
Each confrontation produces a virtuoso display
of evasiveness, of velocity,
a miniature, inconclusive chase.

And it puts me in mind, this probing dance
of our own intimacies,
when finally we get too close,
passing through one another to the other side.

But for years I have had to enter cautiously,
so as not to startle anyone,
to stand in the hallways and call my name,
knock on doors, again announce myself.
I have had to sidle into rooms,
like a child – No, not like a child! Children burst in!
Like a servant, then,
where before I'd entered as of right.

Why, then, should I regret the ending of this?
There is no chance I'd have recovered my former status.
A deteriorating situation is all I'd to look forward to.
Until finally entry would, in any case, have been denied me.

My ultimate exclusion, thus, has been pre-empted by
the one dying and the other selling the house
whose key I still retained.

After the heartfelt appeal,
I arrived on the run,
to find you rummaging among your redcurrent bushes,
pulling out weeds – you scarcely looked up.
I hovered there. Were you embarrassed,
or had you somehow forgotten,
or had you merely needed me to respond,
not to ignore your summons?
Hesitantly, casually, I remarked
that gardening was good therapy,
following this at once with a tactful comment on the evening light.
You enthusiastically agreed – about the light.
You were particularly entranced (sharing it with me)
by those tall foxgloves.
Foxgloves, you recalled, lined the road to your parents'
        summer cottage, near Arundel.
Yes, they grew *wild* there, I said.
It was just, I was struck by the contrast

between natural fecundity and this cultivated urban plot.
Before I could resolve this, you explained:
I'm rediscovering my childhood,
followed by further reflections on the Sussex countryside.
Still I could not reconcile this
with the suburbanness of your garden, even though
the evening light made it glow.
But now as I set down these words of mine,
I see you, attentive, and so purposeful
that I don't know, I don't know.

In India, the dogs kept me awake.
Like a sleepless, occupying army,
no let-up, not until dawn ...

I closed my eyes then, prepared to sleep
a blessed hour or two, when my sparrow couple
flew into the room, chiding and chivying me.

I rose, mysteriously refreshed.

Unbeliever, burdened with this summons,
I waited out the pre-dawn,
longer than any night I'd ever known,
listened to the dogs, the footsteps,
the solipsistic coughing of motors,
and my fellow sleepers turning a deaf ear.

After each cure
we forget our mortality.
Relieved, we again start behaving like fools.
But gradually we come to realize

that actually there are no cures,
and then depression sets in.
We complain endlessly,
agonize in solitude,
daydream,
are preyed upon by charlatans.
But the charlatans ressemble us,
indeed, are even more gullible!
We are the only creatures
who refuse to die,
absolutely refuse.
Hence, all those monuments
we fill the world with.
Even the least of us
does not simply pass away,
even our most evolved religions
express only our inability to remain silent.
Our understanding
advances to within strict limits,
over and over again,
marches up triumphantly
only to be stopped at the border.
And this is where invention starts,
where the imagination takes over,
where the false cures are inaugurated.

In my memory, the rain is suspended,
does not fall. I am
embarrassed on its account.

In my memory, rain sluices
across street and sidewalk,
but where did it come from?

The whole body! The whole body!
In the mind's eye, the *whole* body!

After that, the entire contraption shuffles off.
It is together – if loosely –
and the sounds too
that issue from it, together.

At least, the implication was,
everything was connected.
According to the check we ran,
everything was present and
more or less correct.

I am functioning.
That knowledge seems reliable.
Upright. Though one might wonder too
why not on all fours,
snorting, snuffling
in the grass.

One might wonder,
and in one's imagination
drop to the ground.

Instead, we summon ourselves,
gather ourselves,
assemble ourselves,
erect ourselves.

But sometimes we dream
of sweet grasses,
as, too, of sharp teeth
that click together in our nape.

Are they dreaming, the powers that be,
the powers that were?
Have they been put under a spell?

Meanwhile we are busy,
trying to make the changes irreversible.
We are trundling off all that statuary,
and replacing it with living members,
drawn from among ourselves.

Time stopped,
and our time was substituted for it.

But meanwhile, the old guard
has infiltrated our ranks.
It is trying to invent a new rhetoric
that will permit it to compete on equal terms.
Deprived of its minions,
it has not been deprived of its wits.

It is not incapable of the ultimate sacrifice,
and we are not incapable of the first betrayal.

I never got to school.
True, it happened about me.
Each day I lifted my eye from the pavement,
there it was, happening.
But though I smiled,
though I hid my feelings,
I never got there.

Instead I got here.
Here is where I have always been.
From here, I look back.
I re-read my sentences,
trying to find, to feel, to construct

the connection between them.
I read myself out loud,
with emphasis.

But, for all I know,
I may still be on my way to school.
Yes, perhaps I'm at the beginning,
rather than the end.

———————

Or could it be that, understanding now,
I understand nothing,
as before there was nothing
to understand?

DREAM ALBUM

You were not there at all.
And then I woke.
Why did I recall
that time, during the war,
when I found
a strange boy, red-lipped,
next to me in bed,
even if in the morning he was gone
and again I scoured
the empty beaches on my own?
I reach out
and touch you, turned from me,
oblivious, quite oblivious, of me.

The facade I gestured towards
no longer was! A space,
a space readied for building on,
greeted my unbelieving eyes,
even as my braggart mouth spoke:
"I lived there once – an early Tudor
block of rooms," pointing to
where the window would have been
was mine. That's how I knew
this was a dream, or knew
things were so awry,
it might as well have been.
All other places I'd inhabited
had been pulled down, or eviscerated,
walls, floors, ceilings rearranged.
But this must remain,
which was mine only on loan.

It was a long way down,
a succession of sheer drops, from ledge to ledge,

then wading through breast-high drifts of snow,
snow or water often over my head,
across fathomless fields or torrents of mud,
before the town was again reached ...

I was not dashed in the descent,
from her house, which I had reached before,
by a broad cinder path, easy to negotiate,
offering no vistas, no resplendent views.

But now she was beautiful, that is
the scales, had they not fallen from my eyes?

Not a skateboard,
not, I think, a board on wheels at all,
but a plain board! I am nailed
to a board, since otherwise
I could not stay upright –
though getting to my feet,
with this board attached to them,
is no easy task.

So, perhaps the board's provisional,
or imaginary.
Or perhaps something is written on it,
which will enlighten me.
I do not look. Instead,
I try to imagine what might be written on it.
For sure not: King of the Jews.
Perhaps just the board's maker,
his initials in a corner.

When I am put into a box,
I shall have such a board at my feet.
Maybe I shall leave instructions,
stiff as a board myself,

or wrapped up like a mummy,
that I be set on end.

The world's a deck under my feet.
I balance upon it
and relax into its centre.
I bend my knees,
then spring upwards.
Turf's attached to my soles.
In mid air I awake, boardless.

The old dance palais ... Observing it,
I distance myself from the two women,
stroll ahead of them, then turn aside
to take a closer look.

Pasted to the wall, a photograph
of the cracking porch, Alhambra-style,
left over from the campaign to preserve it ...
I join a group of men, also curious,
and peer through gaps in the fence
into the dark interior. A sweeping staircase,
baroque columns, are what I expect;
instead, there opens before me
a vista of tower blocks, men and machines.
And someone is saying, with a laugh –
bitter or just amused? –
They certainly came on fast ...

Finally I step back, give it a last caressing look,
that old theatre, that old magic-house,
now reduced to a mere facade.
Then I hurry to catch up with the two women,
who have passed it by without a glance.
"I remember it, the old palais," I say to them.
"Magnificent, splendid, it was ..."

I lied, I who had learnt of its existence
only in the nick of time.

Shakespeare said it all.
He was the right man in the right place.
So, isn't it about time I listened!
I lift a corner of the page and peer inside
My heart turns over, or is it my stomach?
Well, that'll do for now! I say to myself.

All my reading life, so far,
I've been putting it off,
but now it seems to me,
perhaps I've been too cautious.
I pick up the book, weigh it, lay it down.
Then I open it, begin to read ...
At once I'm surrounded by voices,
all demanding to be heard at once.
Yes, there's too much simultaneity for me.

So, I'm thinking, thinking!

Perhaps it would be better
to let my hand do the work, let my hand
lift up the cover, leaf through pages.
And then, first, with only half an eye,
only half an ear ... Perhaps.
And to keep talking too,
to keep talking.

It's called, holding one's own.

Love picks his knightly way
through the flesh.

The rustle and slurp of it,
stirred by his passage,
make it impossible to observe
the rules of silence.
Love is surrounded, enthicketed,
beset by danger, he is alert,
his mailed fist hovering above his sword.
But the murmur never exceeds
an inarticulate gurgle.
Only he may not rest,
until he has come to the end of the path.

She was lost. I woke.
Then I went back into the dream to find her.
Went back, back into the dream
to find her. Only not far enough.
I called to her from the edge,
before I had got all the way back,
called to her, before I could see.
I was lazy, over-confident.
And then I realized it was too late,
or too soon,
and instead of going further,
I woke some more.

My mistake was,
that I'd taken it for granted
a gesture was enough,
a symbolic gesture would do.
So I told myself what I thought I knew:
She's not lost really.
But this didn't console me.
I had failed to go back for her,
had called out to her too soon.
The thought that probably
no real harm had been done
didn't console me.

I pick up the phone and dial.
Her voice levels with me.
She tells me to come on over.
I replace the phone, live a little.

That makes me somewhat older than I was!
Maybe I should apologize,
but I don't, and anyway, the change –
you'd hardly notice.

Still, it helps keep us both
just a little stretched.
She gets the gist of it right away,
the unsaid makes for a livelier situation.

She doesn't even object to my setting out on a first trip,
only moments after having arrived.

Where she herself had only dabbed,
I sponged her down with force,
vigorously rubbed, removed the stains.
Encouraged by my care,
she confessed now, sobbing,
that she had thought to end it all.
Unhesitatingly, I showed still more concern,
switched on the light, chiding her gently
for her parsimony.
Yes, I would stay with her,
her need was my excuse,
duty and love no longer burdensome,
gladly assumed, so she might soon rejoice,
whose misery was pure as a child's laugh.

It was left behind,
in propitiation, in lieu maybe
of something dearer?
Not sheer perversity, then,
not lazyness or inertia,
but a kind of superstitiousness
accounts for our failure
to extract from the ruins of our house
the bookcase, that last heirloom, relic ...
Perhaps, it was the price,
or if not the price exactly, the tribute.

I am the weak link in the chain.
For as long as I can remember,
I have been the weak link in the chain.
I am tired of being the weak link in the chain,
in these enduring circumstances, the weak link.
Prisoner, I am the weak link,
your only hope!

I'm up against a wall!
It's a wall presses against my brow,
between my eyes.
I wear it like a small box –
like *tefillin,* for God's sake!
And the sensation descends through my cheekbones
to the roof of my mouth,
and into what's left of my jaw.

Last night, rummaging in Nietzsche's attaché case,
for paper to scribble on,
I came across a pad,

among some notes and a book or two,
evidence of work in progress.
And I flourished one sheet,
showing him both sides,
so he could see it was blank,
and he nodded.

Then I was awake, smiling
in anticipation of the day's work.
Or was it that the great scholar acknowledged me,
for some reason reminding me
of a dear friend and mentor, recently deceased,
that made me smile?

I had been about to tell Nietzsche
that I filled my own bag with at least a month's work,
when I remembered this was no longer true.
So, I said nothing.
Not only because, at that very moment, I awoke,
but also because it would have been perverse,
since, like him, I now carried with me
only what concerned me, day by day.

A new tranquility stretched before,
where it ended not being my concern,
what I would leave behind, not being for me to say.

SELECTED POEMS

Poet with a Violin

He hugged the violin to his breast.
Something broke inside him,
so he couldn't unfold his arms,
he couldn't straighten them
from wrist to chin,
from shoulder to fingers –
to a point in the air.
He stood and hugged himself.
He longed for even one note to float free.

Yom Kippur at the British Museum

Entering the courtyard, I gasped,
seeing a Jew bowler-hatting happily to "shul,"
clasping his prayer-book proudly,
and remembered suddenly –
my wife had thrown it in my way at breakfast ...
breakfast! –
"It's Yom Kippur."

And climbing the steps, my first impulse –
what if I fast three days instead of one,
read the whole prayer-book through,
or go to "shul" on Saturdays –
sickens me. Ach!

And as I sit down it begins.
Enviously I remember that "day off,"
that different day,
when I actually came to love my fellow Jews,
and in general a high point for the year to run up to
and away from.
I sit, hatless and cold,
where today I notice many empty seats,
among students of chess, Portuguese literature,
nuclear strategy, racing horses.
Can I call myself one of the Jews
that I should choose to be in this madhouse,
rather than in that,
on this Day of Days?

But what is the Day of Atonement particularly?
Think! Answer!
It is a day which, by itself, might sustain Jewry,
it is a day encompassing a year,
a day of accounts,

of speculation, resignation, acceptance finally,
a day hot with griefs, joys, fears, hopes,
a day demanding much of an ordinary Jew,
which he could not endure unshared.
How can I, seated under the dome,
hope to make this effort on my own?

Nervous as a solitary hen
my writing flutters on and on.

The trouble is –
while I would not return to the tyranny of the old lion,
I am no emancipated Jew,
nor liberal Jew even.
I am no rationalist, no agnostic.
Rejection of orthodoxy seems to me impertinent –
I cannot take refuge in claiming
that it is on my own account alone –
and now I am afraid to curse God, even in jest;
yet belief does not flower.

Folded over my desk I sit
at the entrance of the synagogue,
contemplating a prayer-shawl,
fingering a prayer-book.
I listen to the old chants in my mind.
Some take me maybe for a beggar.
Bad-tempered beadles beckon me inside.
What can I do except sit
and shake my head?

Fellow Reader

A cough like lace hides his lower face,
a fine-grained briefcase like the wind in feather grass,
a furled umbrella, frail as a fossil spine ....

With what elegance and poise
Old Age vibrates above the chair and sits,
composing himself with least disturbance of the atmosphere,
as though adjusting a picture on the wall.

Man at Work

The great sky is laughing at me.
I stare at it. Yes, I too can see the joke!
I cast a few words onto the page,
stir them around,
fixing whatever pattern occurs,
lifting it, revolving it in the light.
Is this work for a man?
My wife brings me a sandwich,
glancing suspiciously at my idle hands.
I feed, turning with greasy fingers
the fifteen short poems
I've fabricated in as many days,
each begging to be unmade.
But they are all I have to show.

The great sky has forgotten me –
it has forgotten everything.
I brush the crumbs from my notebook onto the table.
My head feels like a cork wedged tight into a bottle.
How to relieve the pressure?
I look out of the window for signs in nature.
Nature gives me none.
I register only my own obtuse presence.
I lay my cheek on the crumb-strewn table,
listen to the endless chatter of the children.

I wait.

At the appropriate moment I rise
and go into the kitchen to lend a hand.

Memories of War

In this green and pleasant land,
where V1s and V2s
were not aimed specifically at Jews,
I played Nazis, Nasties
on the bombed sites.

We collected shit-colored, sky-fallen metal.
My stomach still turns from the time
I picked up a bit of shit instead ...

But why here and not
Lodz, Warsaw, Brussels, Paris?
I went on growing.
With nostalgia, I remember
"Onward Christian Soldiers" and
"To be a Pilgrim."

A Businessman

He was homo trilinguis: Hebrew, Greek and Latin.
This learning remained with him,
a kind of curse, an anachronism.
He loved Classical Greece and found the contemporary world
      wanting,
and lovingly he recalled the barbarous legends of the Hebrews.
Yeshiva bokhur, Classical scholar,
he'd a memory would let nothing go –
time simply had no effect on it.
After thirty years in knitwear,
he still construed Virgil with ease,
as comprehensively and tediously as he explained
the significance and symbolism of the Passover.
Though he could have afforded it many times over,
he never visited Greece, or the Holy Land.
Instead, photographs show him
on the terrace in Monte Carlo,
in tennis slacks at Riva Bella,
or sitting stiffly in a deckchair,
squinting up at the sun in Bournemouth.
I know it's presumptuous to say so,
but if he'd been able to lay down his burden of knowledge,
he'd probably have been better off.

Scenes of Family Life

Once, at table, my father's glass eye fell out.
He said "Ach!" and reached beneath the table,
searching as best he could
with one hand clapped over the socket.

Our second-cousin Zelig, the pig farmer,
in unexplained circumstances,
had lost one plump finger during the war.
Laughable almost, when set beside other horrors,
it was enough to queer my relationship with him.

There was a blind lady, a distant relative as well,
who turned up for all the family occasions,
including, of course, my barmitzvah.
I took her hand and she smiled at my brow.
I smiled too, glassily staring at her wrinkled décolleté.

After the Death

You pulled back the sheet –
such familiarity, aunt! –
and beamed. "Comme il est beau,
papa," you said.
Still awed by that final breath of his,
all I heard was "papa."
And, yes, I thought, it's true
this was my dad,
if only because at last
he has gone before,
as fathers should.

Father's Anniversary

August –
and it's hot, as on the day you were buried.
We walk stiffly up the long path,
identify the row, stop
before your double bed-sized slab.

Now, as each year, I try to think of you,
to form a prayer,
suppressing the faint impulse to shout.

She stoops. She places a pebble on your slab,
then raises her head:
she spells out the inscription on the stone,
as though confronted by it for the first time.
Doing duty for you who lie there,
she interprets the Hebrew letters.
We cough, murmur, and nod.
We do not look at one another –
there's this to look at.
Finally, she turns –
too soon for me, though nothing's to be gained by staying.
Heads bowed, we file back to the path,
leave you to yourself.

Returning to the car park,
absently – irreverently? – we read
the inscriptions carved on other stones.
Resigned yet at the same time shocked,
we note, as always,
how the dead have increased
since our last visit.

In the back seat,
she shuts her eyes.

She slumps, not so much overcome
as conserving herself.
In front, slowly,
we loosen our collars,
remove our skull caps,
roll down the windows.

The Wound

In the dark something stirs.
I bend to touch it.
Something soft, feathery.
A bird?
A nestling – fluffy, baby-big.
Bigger than a sparrow.
A pigeon maybe,
a thrush.
No, I'm sure it's a little dove,
a pet for my child.
With trembling hand I reach for it –
it shuffles free.
But it doesn't fly off.
Why doesn't it fly off?
What is it doing here in this dark?
Wounded?
At the thought, my hand recoils.

Blunt jaws like pliers close round a finger.
I shake the sudden appendage.
The jaws hold fast.
What is this thing?
A rat maybe?
Then why no pain?
I shake and shake and finally it flies off –
like another hand.

In the light I study my finger,
examine it carefully
for blood,
for mark of tooth,
for anything at all.

The Cry

I stand in the hallway,
in the clamor of the town beyond these walls –
the walls, too, thunder.
There are explosions even nearer.
Swivelling my head, I listen hard,
trying to pinpoint them.
When a child's cough comes clear,
I start and the floor yelps.
I hold my breath then and listen harder.
It's an infant's cry now reaches out for me
over the pandemonium of the sleeping household;
it draws me to where, unsmiling, she stares up.
My moonface floats into position,
her panicky eyes search for the borders of mine.

Idyll

The baby watches the coverlet twitching in its fists.
A horse looks through the window.
Mother is putting currants into a cake.
In the garden an ant-hill seems to be ripening.

If someone were to play a violin, it would not be right.
If someone were to read a poem, it would not be right.
If someone were to clear his throat, it would not be right.

Moth

A moth falls like a dead leaf,
scraping against the wall at my bedside,
springing up and away as it hits the bed,
butting its soft head tremendously
against an endless series of walls,
or jagging into the light
until, in a dead faint,
it falls again, spinning like a streamer,
to spring away from the floor this time,
or stagger drunkenly about it.

I have watched moths rest against the wall
like chips of wood.
I have admired their dun elegance,
the watermarked wings,
while shrinking from their ambivalent touch,
the threat of them in the air.

Out of bed!
I bat the furry bodies of moths with a folded newspaper,
I crumple them on the wing,
I shiver their frail timber,
I shed their glittering blood,
I will not let them possess me.

And after it is over,
I tread cautiously on bare feet
over the dim lino where something flutters –
back to bed.

Poem

The prayer grew cold.
The prayer of her body
stiffened beyond reach.
All the breath went out of her,
she melted into hell fumes,
kneeling there four days and nights,
a cigarette burnt out against her fingers.

There was none to put his arms about this child
that first night,
and in the morning,
as the sun lit her head,
none to gaze at her,
to smooth her hair.
She knelt on, rotting in her clothes.

And so it continued for three more days and nights.

There can be no celebrating this death,
no resplendent "refusal to mourn."

The White Cat

for Sue

Not albino but a tender white,
with a face like a little girl's.
And a stillness ... Well,
all cats are still,
but she'd find the still center of places too,
and settle, as though on air,
as though slightly elevated above the floor,
as though it had been foreordained, directed by another
     intelligence
that had made her white, a luminosity, one of its angels.

She was floating like that when I first encountered her,
at the altar-center of an empty room,
like a small god, or a meditator,
but with wide-open eyes.
It was dusk and I found myself wondering:
Are cats all over the world
sitting like this in empty rooms,
waiting for someone to speak through them,
living transmitters, gathered at the appointed moment
throughout the world? She seemed
not so much communicating,
as part of a network of communicants.

Summer, and I sat at dawn on the stone steps to the garden,
and she came to me out of the deep garden,
traversing slats of sunlight,
inspected me, then sat at a little distance,
half turned away, as though
interceding with someone.

Later, for as many nights
as it took my friend to die,
I'd see a luminescence in the garden,
unhidden in the long grass.

Changing Sky

The saturated hedgerow brushes my coat.
Sheep graze in the downpour
or lie with lifted head.

Soft-footed, the rain enters the earth.
My eye is caught by the glitter of an abandoned web.
I look across to where trees cling
to a glowing hill line.

Paris Stripped Bare of her Rats

Under every Paris is the fact of rats.
Lift Paris
and the rats,
paling in the light,
perish.

The sewer dries in their throats,
the dark blood shrivels,
flies stick in the smooth pelts.

And the children of sunlight,
who put on clean shirts every day,
climb into their glass heavens,
their bellies warm,
their hair tossing unmatted,
everything scabrous slipped out of.

A Dream of Tall Buildings

I used to have a recurrent dream.
An immigrant, approaching New York,
I'd see its towering skyline
and suddenly feel warm, happy, fulfilled.
Now, New York's baroque cliffs have mostly turned to glass.
Yet that dream still inspires me.
My immigrant blood yearns
for the promise of the nineteenth century.

So English

When I was a child, I knew kids like you,
I wanted to be like them,
to grow up like them,
not The Wandering Jew.
But evidently it takes two generations.

Later I emigrated to America.
Of course I'd no hope ever of arriving,
but I left you, my children,
and the me who was becoming just a bit like you,
so English.

Departure

Still I long
for those grey London walks of ours,
the swings,
your cool demand:
"Push me on the swings!"

Already you can push yourself.
You do.
Through me you arch
and, watching, I
am sliced in two!

To sit for ever
on a bench with you
is all I ask.
But soon you're saying:
"Take me home now,
take me home!"

Winter

The flies' strength has diminished to nothing.
Sapless, without sheen, they die,
by negative weight adhering to the ceiling.

Looking along my nose's length,
I notice a fly on my sweater,
dead.

A slow pat dislodges flies from the air,
or plummets them from walls.

They are old, so old.

Autodidact

Piece by piece I assemble my New Life.
Disregarding accusations of hypocrisy,
I learn to care by going through the motions.
In the end, to each I shall give
my undivided attention.

Change

I am trying to remember ...
The two trees outside the house
(they mentioned them in a letter)
were green when I arrived.
I can't recall what they looked like
three months ago ...it's been a long autumn.
The leaves of course are pale now,
a few of them still hanging tissuelike,
sodden with all the snow they've drifted through.
I cling to the passing days,
resist as tenaciously, as unavailingly, as the leaves.
And tonight I keep bobbing out to sniff the snow,
to feel the cold, to absorb the whiteness,
in short, to get it into my head
and accept it in my body.

I wonder, was this why, as a child,
I began to write poems,
talking endlessly to myself,
exhorting myself to accept the passing of time?
This year has been worse than ever:
never have I been less eager
to greet the future.
Therefore, I cling not to the present, but the past,
concentrating on a point
in an ideal, static past.
Paradise is everything I have ever experienced,
simultaneously, unalterably fixed –
a choir, a single reverberating chord,
my entire multiple self assembled,
in order and harmony.

I do not fear death, but incompleteness, unpreparedness.
It is my great ambition to be ready,
to know I have fulfilled myself!
Meanwhile, what I attempt is beyond my grasp.
The alternation of the seasons continues to torment me –
the mutation of bodies,
the instability of individual destinies,
the fluctuation of relationships.

I do not pace myself through life
but stumble after one thing and another,
taking the unalterableness of change
as evidence of my inevitable failure.

As my impotence unfolds,
I move towards inertia.
I pray that there is some purpose,
I pray that I shall grow wise
in measure as my folly spends itself,
so that I shall be prepared to take charge
when its bankruptcy is final.

Rehearsal

You were in my arms when a dear friend called
and held me with his distant voice.
Fifteen minutes I walked the room,
the phone pressed hard against my face.

A premonition of the end?
Our evening calm and then the slack
of time jerked tight,
though we came together again, our world

was back in place. We held on fast
with legs, and arms, and mouths, and eyes,
and fell away into sleep at last,
as close as we'd ever got.

I start as the alarm rings up
the curtain on a whitewashed sky.
But we wake together slowly, feel
the darkness in our warm limbs die.

You leave. The thunderous prison silence
of your absence swallows up all sound.
I rehearse, abruptly shut the door,
and you rehearse not looking round.

Volte-Face

I go through the motions.
We laugh together, but afterwards
there is silence. Not just nothing to say –
an active, positive, final silence!

Before, it was your indifference pained me,
now it's my own,
the despair of seeking and not finding,
replaced by the despair of being sought and not found.

From Aegina

Allow me to write you a line or two,
not a really long poem –
I leave that kind of thing to you –
and no metaphors with Greece in them, I promise ...

For I shall always recall your compassionate mockery,
and immediately following, ingenuously, the seriousness
of your deep sure-footed voice, used to negotiating crags,
that flawlessly,
with the confidence of accomplished oratory,
of ritual dance,
demonstrates the force and equilibrium
of the Man-God.
And your dark sober eyes too,
at the same time regarding me, I love and honor –
See, I am using words out of the marriage ceremony!
And your vulnerability,
your face that seems to turn upward,
as if waiting for someone's brutal palm to press it down;
that seems to say:
I can take it, and besides
I have no choice! –
your absolute vulnerability, constituting toughness,
because you have no choice,
and know it –

You explode at the foolhardiness of some new adventure,
some new jousting with the forces out to get you.
And how I shall miss your telling of this, so unaccountable ...

Levée

The sun has slept without clothes.
Now, as it prepares its simple toilet,
you wait grimly.
A thin haze already covers the sky.
The sun, its robe spread carelessly about its nakedness,
flaps towards you – already it is airborne.
The earth crouches, shrinking away from it,
grumbling, complaining *sotto voce*,
as the sun climbs, always too close,
crawls over it like a monkey,
with prehensile hands and feet.
The wind scurries about,
searching for freshness,
exhausting itself –
it'll die anyway.
Impatiently you brush aside
its touch that crawls over you,
like the sun over the sky.
It fingers you,
musses your moist hair.
The sun meanwhile crowns you from the neck up,
your whole head,
as though you'd thrust it in a lion's jaws.
You keep damned still!

Missing Part

Part of me is gone.
I enter my second half century,
a bit missing.
A section was marked,
cut loose, taken away,
leaving a memory behind.
I cherish that.
Late at night, in the small hours,
I imagine myself whole again.
Oh, what a longing fills me!

Yet this had to do with learning too –
which is why,
when I now consider that airy gap,
and even though I try nostalgically to fill it,
I am not so deeply saddened.
Part of me was taken away
and I was sewn up again,
a bagful of bones less a bit.
To summarize, one of my corners was cut,
one of my angles suppressed,
and I was patched together,
not quite as good as new,
but with a built-in aide-memoire,
better than any knot-tied handkerchief.

I've a fellow feeling now for the twisted and the torn,
for the wheelchair brigade,
the sweepers and the tappers.
The hole in me's my badge of honorary membership in that club.
There's an easier way through me than there was.
I'm skewed, like a Picasso.

But late at night and sometimes early in the morning,
I imagine myself as I was –
like some young girl,
who dares to dress up only in those solitary hours!
Was I sparing the hurt world my flawless beauty then?
Had I simply disgused myself,
so I might pass for one of suffering humanity?

Stop! The past's off bounds!
If I cannot forget that raid –
a hostage taken, never to be returned –
I've paid too much for my hold on the present,
for the right to move on.
As one does, I just left a piece of me behind,
a token I was there.

Helen's House

Winter has passed.
The winter of her death has passed.
The peonies in the garden have raised their standards;
lilly-of-the-valley nudges through last year's litter;
the buckeye buds stand erect like light bulbs;
rhubarb shows leaf, and the old vine looks alert.
But the bird-bath her side of the lawn
is untended now – she intended,
she intended to be here;
I can feel it.

Perhaps that is why it's so hard to write a poem for her?
It is as though she watched me trying to write it,
wondering how to address me –
Dan, Daniel, Danny – she never knew –
What's that you're doing?
Writing your elegy, Helen ...

Each day I stare at her square house,
filled now with tenants,
the house she lived in nearly all her life,
twenty-five years of it on her own, after Dutch died,
knowing that since she was unready to leave,
she is still busying herself inside,
putting things away, checking the locks,
and at night looking out of her window at the lights in ours.
She kept a bell to summon us should anything go wrong.
Silly, isn't it! she apologized.

But perhaps she was not so unready.
Perhaps her ghost is not so restless as I imagine.
It seems that as she lay dying in Mercy,
she suddenly asked: What is a haven?
And the one sitting by her bedside explained:
A safe place, Helen.
And she nodded.

How Death Came About

1.
When God created life he created death too,
but seeing what a good time was being had by all,
he hadn't the heart to let it loose.
Instead he visited people with boils and sores,
with the plague which would have carried them off wholesale,
with domestic strife, which drove many to the brink,
until they cried out: Lord, Lord, relieve our suffering!
Whereupon God sent death to them,
in answer to their prayers.

2.
The man Adam said to his wife Emily,
My dear, since we agreed always to be honest with one another,
I have to tell you there's this woman Eve ...
But Emily didn't let him finish.
She had been afraid of this from the start
and now she began to heap curses on Adam, Eve,
and above all on God, who had assigned her the role
    of eternal sufferer and victim,
abandoned wife and ...
well, at least there weren't any kids.

Eve, cold-eyed, was meanwhile waiting in the wings,
wearing a sheath dress and nothing on underneath.
God regretted having started the whole business,
he couldn't stand the woman's tears.
For the first time he wished there were a higher authority
    he could refer the matter to.
Finally, he laid a mighty finger on Emily's trembling shoulder.

Child, he whispered earthshatteringly,
I admit I made a mistake.
To save you from further humiliation and suffering,
I shall take ... No! shrieked Emily, but too late.
Eve sauntered into the room. Adam wept.

Nobody Will Listen

Nobody will listen to her.
What she wants to say is:
I'd like you to make me strong again,
I'd like you to make me agile again –
but above all, take away the fog!
"Forget the rest. Just take
the fog away!" she says.
"It's old age, dear," they explain.
They no longer tell her how young she looks.
"You'll have to learn to live with it."
They are really not helpful –
they're not prepared to discuss it.
Nobody will listen to her.

Pity the Poor Racist

Pity the poor racist,
the poor purist,
who not only found red men here
but was almost at once inundated
by the diverse dusky hordes from Europe,
particularly those Jews, with their dangling arms,
soon busy snipping and gesticulating.

Pity him
whose monolingual, New World dream
turned into a nightmare, a synthetic babble of voices,
that he was not able to erect barriers,
that diversity became a creed,
that the idea of universal refuge instead of refuge for the elect
prevailed – pity him.

To know that all men were created equal,
only if by 'all' you mean 'us,'
and then to be obliged to compete and negotiate with 'them,'
for they are legion –
oh pity him, though he
is without pity.

Summoning the Dead

I rapped on a board –
actually, it must have been The Book of the Dead,
lying on my bedside table –
and alerted one of them.
Are they standing in line
that as soon as he came through
I knew who it must be!
Jacques, in this case.
But the voice never quite became a voice,
and the presence was more in the mind
than in the air.
In despair I put my question:
How are you? with the emphasis on 'are,'
neutral then but concerned as well,
quiet, soft, tentative –
it was just an opening gambit, and still
he faded, if you can call it fading,
when something's scarcely there at all.
He faded, as a thought goes from your head
and cannot for a while be got in mind again.
I continued to tap,
but now each tap only reinforced his absence –
until I woke.
The tapping continued for a few moments longer,
an echo, or as though
someone were signalling me.

Peonies Again

The peonies are on the march again.
There's no more room for them under ground.
Spearpoints break surface,
Specks of color in the crumbling dirt.
I stop to examine this upthrust
at the bottom of the garden,
this promise of future order in a wasteland,
order and organization, as though someone
sat and planned it all in a notebook,
this rising straight up from the ground,
the sap busy in them.
And the tight promise of these tips,
swelling to cupolas,
rounding into globes,
tight fistfulls, bunched, bales,
packed like golfballs.
And the stems starting to tilt.
And then the black ants come to these oozing earths,
make passes across them as though urging them on,
milking, them milking them,
until their resolve snaps! They split apart, unfurl.
Like a great sigh.
The stems sink lower, lower,
as rank on rank of petals unpack themselves ...

Not this year.
They are laying a parking strip there,
at the bottom of the garden.
Meanwhile, I stoop and easily spot them still,
only their tips showing among great clods,
cans, boxes, brittle scraps of paper from the alley.
"We're back again!" they are saying.
"We'll soon get things straightened out here."

And you can almost feel the earth tremble from their upthrust.
But this year is not like other years.
This years diggers and concrete-layers are bringing order,
and cars with their snouts and staring eyes
will assemble where peonies gave their color to the air.

Rabbits in the Garden

We've rabbits in the garden.
How did they get here?
They lie, like boats at anchor,
one pair, then two, three,
long streaks of greyness, with alert ears
tuned to the distant grassy slopes.
Their haven's a stack of tires, or the wood pile.
Their young are being picked off by our cats.

Wearying finally of tiny corpses,
of torn-off booties and bunny guts strewn wide
by these indifferent eaters,
we lock the cats in.
Now the house periodically fills with mewing,
as the two predators pace,
before returning to their unearned rest.

Meanwhile the rabbits, more and more
take silent possession of their half acre,
listening to the wind,
not to the rumble and whine of traffic,
seeing grass tips,
not the unbending face of office block and parking ramp.

Still as boats on a calm sea,
all they have is their antennae,
stirred by the breeze,
in still, calm panic.

Our fat grey cat has given up.
But our slim black one still whirls on the kitchen floor,
loosing her large Siamese yowls.
She stalks past me, gazing reproachfully,

then gallops back to the door,
rears, stretching her body,
stares out with that inward, listening look.

Looking out myself,
I see a rabbit propel itself vertically upwards,
five feet into the air!

Protest

"You see, I'm very fond of trees ..." said I
to the retired man who had been cutting down trees in his yard,
and had just cut one down on the border with ours.
I tried to stop him, crying:
"Excuse me sir, excuse me sir! ..."
But of course he couldn't hear over the scream of his chainsaw.
Now he and his wife squatted on the slope of the gully,
listening to my futile remarks.
They gazed wide-eyed, in sympathetic understanding.
"So are we," he said, nodding vigorously,
and then explained that the trees were so close together
they didn't grow right, just tall –
"Like a pole," he said, pointing at the fallen tree –
and that he was going to plant new trees.
They too valued their privacy, wanted to be screened from our
house, as we did from theirs –
I shrugged politely.
"We're thinking of a willow," he said speculatively.
"It gives a lots of shade and is fast growing."
Even disarmed as I was by their mildness, I wondered ...
Fast? How fast? Five, ten, twenty years? ...
Later it occurred to me, too, how anachronistic
    a willow would be here,
where what grew naturally was a tangle of scrubby oak,
    box-elder, locust, and mulberry –
"Messy trees," his wife had called these last.
His expression and hers, full of solicitude,
was unchanged all the time we talked.
They heard me out, as you'd listen to someone who'd got hold of
the wrong end of the stick,
who hadn't quite understood it was for the best,
but maybe was just beginning to,
and with a little patience ...

They wanted all their trees to be full, with plenty of light and air, not crowded, intertwining, struggling for *lebensraum*.
They wanted all the death and dying to be dragged out into the open and taken away ...
This morning the tree was chopped up, piled neatly on the sidewalk, like a funeral pyre, alongside the garbage cans.
And I remembered with a pang
that moment when his saw ended its life,
with me helplessly crying,
"Excuse me sir, excuse me sir!"

A beetle carefully explores
the window pane.
It probes it, inch by inch,
with total concentration,
with unfailing expectation
of a favorable outcome.

DANIEL WEISSBORT was born in 1935, in London. He was educated at St. Paul's School, Queens' College, Cambridge and later at the London School of Economics where he studied Soviet literary politics. In 1965, with Ted Hughes, he founded the journal *Modern Poetry in Translation*, which he still edits and which is now published by King's College, London. Before coming to America in 1973, he published two collections of his own poetry and a number of volumes of poetry translated from the Russian. His *Post-War Russian Poetry* was published in 1974 and *Russian Poetry: The Modern Period* in 1978. A new and expanded edition of the latter, *Twentieth Century Russian Poetry*, appeared in 1992, as did *The Poetry of Survival: Post-War Poets of Central and Eastern Europe*. He has also translated, from the French, work by Goncourt-winner Patrick Modiano and Nobel-winner Claude Simon, and has edited a collection of essays, *Translating Poetry: The Double Labyrinth*. Weissbort has published two further volumes and two chapbooks of his own poetry, as well as a number of collections of translated poetry, since coming to America. Since 1974, he has directed the Translation Workshop at the University of Iowa, where he is a professor of English and Comparative Literature.